C Programming Wizardry: From Zero to Hero in 10 Days

: C Programming Wizardry: From Zero to Hero in 10 Days

Copyright © 2023 by Teo Kok Keong

Inquiries should be addressed to:
teokk@knowledgeclique,biz

Introduction

Welcome to the enchanting world of C programming! We're absolutely delighted that you've embarked on this incredible journey with us, from ground zero to becoming a wizard in C programming, all in just 10 days.

C, often referred to as the "mother of all programming languages," is a timeless and potent tool in the realm of computer programming. It's the language that has laid the foundation for countless software systems, operating systems, and applications. In the next 10 days, you will traverse a path that will take you from a complete novice to a proficient C programmer.

Whether you aspire to embark on a career in software development, enhance your programming skills, or simply want to explore the intricate world of C, this course is meticulously designed to provide you with the knowledge and practical skills you need.

Each day of this course is thoughtfully structured to offer you step-by-step guidance, hands-on exercises, and a nurturing learning environment. I will accompany you on this fascinating 10-day journey. Get ready to wield the magic of C programming and unleash your inner coding wizard!

Please follow Knowledge Clique FB page to access all the exercises code an support from the Author. FB page link https://www.facebook.com/knowledgeclique

All the code listed in this book will be freely available in Github. The link will be provided in the Knowledge Clique FB page.

Happy learning!

Sincerely,
Teo kok keong

Table of Contents

Day 1 Introduction to C Programming

Day 1 Introduction to C Programming

Reading Assignment What is C Programming?

C programming is a powerful and versatile computer programming language that has played a pivotal role in shaping the world of software development. Created in the early 1970s by Dennis Ritchie at Bell Labs, C has since become one of the most widely used and influential programming languages in the world. But what exactly is C programming, and why is it so important?

At its core, C is a general-purpose programming language known for its efficiency, flexibility, and portability. Here's what sets it apart:

1. Efficiency: C is renowned for its ability to produce highly efficient and fast-running programs. Its low-level capabilities allow developers to control hardware resources directly, making it an ideal choice for system-level programming, embedded systems, and applications where performance is critical.

2. Flexibility: C is a versatile language that supports both high-level and low-level programming. It offers a rich set of data types, operators, and control structures, giving programmers the freedom to express complex algorithms and manipulate data with precision.

3. Portability: C programs can be written to work on various platforms and operating systems with minimal modification. This portability is essential for creating software that can run on different computers, from desktop PCs to smartphones and embedded devices.

4. Modularity: C promotes modular programming, allowing developers to break down complex projects into smaller, manageable pieces called functions. This makes code more organized, easier to understand, and simpler to maintain.

5. Large Standard Library: C comes with a vast standard library that provides a wide range of functions for tasks like file handling, memory management, and input/output operations. This library simplifies common programming tasks and reduces the need to reinvent the wheel.

6. Legacy and Endurance: C's enduring popularity is a testament to its reliability and longevity. Many operating systems, including Unix and Linux, are written in C. Countless software applications, from web browsers to video games, contain C code or use libraries written in C.

C programming is an excellent choice for aspiring programmers and experienced developers alike. Learning C not only equips you with a solid foundation in programming but also opens doors to various career opportunities in software development, systems programming, game development, and more.

In summary, C programming is a versatile and efficient language with a rich history and a bright future. It continues to be an essential tool in the world of technology, enabling developers to create software that powers our digital world.

Setting Up Your Development Environment

Before you embark on your journey into the world of C programming, it's essential to set up a development environment that allows you to write, compile, and run your C programs efficiently. Here are the key steps to get you started:

1. Choose a Text Editor or Integrated Development Environment (IDE):

The first decision you'll need to make is selecting a text editor or an integrated development environment (IDE) for writing your C code. Some popular options include:

- **Visual Studio Code (VS Code):** A highly customizable and free code editor with C/C++ extensions.

- **Code::Blocks:** A free, open-source IDE specifically designed for C/C++ development.
- **Eclipse:** A versatile IDE that supports C/C++ development with various plugins available.
- **Dev-C++:** A simple and lightweight IDE for Windows users.

Choose the one that suits your preferences and platform.

2. Install a C Compiler:

To compile your C programs into executable files, you'll need a C compiler. One of the most commonly used C compilers is GCC (GNU Compiler Collection). The installation process varies depending on your operating system:

- **Linux:** GCC is often pre-installed. If not, you can install it using your package manager (e.g., `sudo apt install gcc` on Ubuntu).
- **Windows:** You can use MinGW (Minimalist GNU for Windows) to get GCC on Windows. Install MinGW and select the C and C++ compilers during installation.
- **macOS:** You can install GCC using the Xcode Command Line Tools, which you can get from the Mac App Store or by running `xcode-select --install` in the terminal.

3. Verify Your Installation:

To ensure that your C compiler is correctly installed, open a terminal or command prompt and type:

gcc --version

You should see information about the installed GCC version. This verifies that the compiler is ready for use.

4. Create a Workspace:

Organize your C projects by creating a dedicated workspace folder on your computer. This will help keep your projects organized and make it easier to manage your files.

5. Start Writing Code:

With your development environment set up, you're ready to start writing C code. Create a new C source file (typically with a `.c` extension) in your workspace and begin your programming journey.

Setting up your development environment is the first step towards becoming proficient in C programming. Once you're set up, you can dive into the world of coding, learning the language's syntax, and building increasingly complex and powerful programs.

Hand on Exercise 1: Setup code::block

Int this exercise, we willi install Code::Blocks and write a "Hello, World!" program in C on a Windows system:

Step 1: Download Code::Blocks

1. Open your web browser and go to the official Code::Blocks website:
http://www.codeblocks.org/downloads.
 Note: that the web is fast changing and the link might be outdated, you could instead google for the latest link.

2. Under the "Downloads" section, click on "Download the binary release."

3. Choose the "codeblocks-xx.xxmingw-setup.exe" version (where xx.xx is the version number). This version includes the Code::Blocks IDE along with the MinGW compiler for Windows.

4. Click the download link to start the download. Save the installer to your computer.

Step 2: Install Code::Blocks

1. Locate the downloaded "codeblocks-xx.xxmingw-setup.exe" file and double-click on it to run the installer.

2. You will see a "Code::Blocks Setup Wizard" window. Click "Next" to begin the installation process.

3. Accept the license agreement by selecting "I Agree" and click "Next."

4. Choose the installation directory for Code::Blocks. The default location is usually fine, so you can click "Next."

5. Select the components to install. Ensure that "Code::Blocks" and "MinGW" are selected. You can leave other options at their default settings and click "Next."

6. Choose the Start Menu folder for shortcuts and click "Next."

7. Select the additional tasks if desired (e.g., creating desktop and quick launch icons). Click "Next."

8. Review your choices, and when you're ready, click "Install" to begin the installation process.

9. Wait for the installation to complete. This may take a few minutes.

10. Once the installation is finished, you will see a "Completing the Code::Blocks Setup Wizard" screen. Check the box that says "Run Code::Blocks" and click "Finish."

Step 3: Write the "Hello, World!" Program

1. Code::Blocks should now be open. To create a new project, click on "File" in the top menu and select "New" > "Project..."

2. In the "New Project" dialog, select "Console application" and click "Go."

3. Choose "C" as the programming language and click "Next."

4. Give your project a name, such as "HelloWorld," and choose a directory to save it in. Click "Next."

5. Ensure that "Create 'Debug' configuration" is selected and click "Finish."

6. In the Code::Blocks IDE, you will see a new project workspace. On the left, you'll have a "Sources" folder. Inside that, you'll see a file named "main.c." Double-click on it to open it.

7. Replace the existing code with the following "Hello, World!" program:

```c
#include <stdio.h>

int main() {
    printf("Hello, World!\n");
    return 0;
}
```

8. Save the file by clicking "File" > "Save" or pressing Ctrl + S.

Step 4: Compile and Run the Program

1. Click on the "Build" menu and select "Build and Run" (or simply press F9).

2. Code::Blocks will compile your program and execute it. You should see the "Hello, World!" message displayed in the console at the bottom of the IDE.

Congratulations! You've successfully installed Code::Blocks on Windows and written and executed your first C program.

```
C:\myproject\t1\t1\bin\Debug    ×    +    ∨

Hello world!

Process returned 0 (0x0)    execution time : 0.023 s
Press any key to continue.
```

Figure 1 Example of a console output of the execution of hello World program

Note that Code:: Block will be the default IDE use throughout this book.

Day 2: Basic Concepts

Day 2: Basic Concepts

Reading Assignment: Variables and Data Types

In the world of programming, variables are like the building blocks that allow you to store and manipulate data. Understanding variables and data types is fundamental to mastering the C programming language. In this chapter, we will explore the concept of variables, learn about different data types, and understand how to declare and use them in C.

What Are Variables?

A variable is a named storage location in a computer's memory where you can store data. These named storage locations can hold different types of information, such as numbers, characters, and more. Variables allow you to work with data in your programs by giving it a meaningful name and a place in memory.

Declaring Variables

Before you can use a variable in C, you need to declare it. Declaration tells the compiler the variable's name and data type, which is crucial for allocating the right amount of memory. Here's the basic syntax for declaring a variable:

data_type variable_name;

For example, to declare an integer variable named `age`, you would use:

int age;

Data Types in C

C offers a variety of data types that allow you to store different kinds of data. Some of the common data types include:

int: Used for storing integers (whole numbers), e.g., `int age = 25;`

float: Used for storing floating-point numbers (numbers with decimals), e.g., `float price = 19.99;`

char: Used for storing single characters, e.g., `char grade = 'A';`

double: Used for storing double-precision floating-point numbers, e.g., `double pi = 3.14159265359;`

Bool: Used for storing Boolean values (`true` or `false`), e.g.,
Bool isStudent = 1;

void: Used for indicating that a function does not return a value, e.g., `void myFunction();`

Initializing Variables

When you declare a variable, you can also initialize it, which means assigning an initial value to the variable. Here's how you can declare and initialize variables:

int score = 100;
float temperature = 98.6;
char grade = 'A';

Variable Naming Rules

In C, variable names must follow certain rules:

Variable names are case-sensitive, meaning `myVariable` and `myvariable` are considered different.

Variable names can consist of letters, digits, and underscores but must start with a letter or underscore.

Reserved words (keywords) like `int`, `float`, or `char` cannot be used as variable names.

Variable names should be meaningful and reflect the purpose of the variable.

Understanding variables and data types is essential as you begin your journey into C programming. Variables allow you to store and manipulate data, and data types determine what kind of data you can work with. In the next chapter, we'll explore how to assign values to variables, perform operations on them, and delve deeper into the world of C programming.

Reading Assignment: Input and Output

Programming without input and output is like having a conversation without listening or speaking. In this chapter, we will explore how to receive input from users, display output to the screen, and interact with the world outside your program in C. Input and output (I/O) are essential aspects of any programming language, and C provides a powerful set of tools for handling them.

Standard Input and Output

In C, we use the Standard Input (`stdin`) and Standard Output (`stdout`) to perform input and output operations. `stdin` represents the keyboard as the source of input, while `stdout` represents the screen as the destination for output. These streams are associated with the console by default.

Output using printf()

The `printf()` function is a fundamental tool for displaying output in C. It allows you to format and display text and data on the screen. Here's a basic example:

```c
#include <stdio.h>
```

```
int main() {
    printf("Hello, World!\n");
    return 0;
}
```

- *printf()* is a library function defined in `<stdio.h>`.
- `"\n"` is an escape sequence for a newline character.

Input using scanf()

The `scanf()` function is used to read input from the user. It is also part of the `<stdio.h>` library. Here's an example of how to use `scanf()`:

```
#include <stdio.h>

int main() {
    int age;
    printf("Enter your age: ");
    scanf("%d", &age);
    printf("You are %d years old.\n", age);
    return 0;
}
```

- `%d` is a format specifier for an integer.
- `&age` is the address of the `age` variable, which allows `scanf()` to store the input value there.

Formatted Input and Output

C provides various format specifiers for different data types:

- `%d` for integers
- `%f` for floating-point numbers
- `%c` for characters
- `%s` for strings

- `%lf` for double-precision floating-point numbers

File Input and Output

C also supports file I/O operations, allowing you to read from and write to files. You can use functions like `fopen()`, `fprintf()`, `fscanf()`, and `fclose()` to work with files.

Input and output are fundamental concepts in programming, and mastering them is essential for creating useful and interactive programs. In this chapter, we've introduced you to the basics of input and output in C using `printf()` and `scanf()`. In the next chapter, we'll dive deeper into control structures and decision-making, which are crucial for creating more sophisticated programs.

Hand on exercise 1: Declare and initialize variables of different data types

Variable Declarations and Initializations

Integer Variables: Declare and initialize two integer variables, num1 and num2, with values of your choice.

Floating-Point Variables: Declare and initialize two floating-point variables, float1 and float2, with values of your choice.

Character Variables: Declare and initialize two character variables, char1 and char2, with characters of your choice.

String Variables: Declare and initialize a string variable, name, with your name or any other string.

Boolean Variable: Declare and initialize a boolean variable, isProgrammingFun, and set it to 1 if you find programming fun or 0 if you don't.

Display Values: Print out the values of all the variables using printf statements. For example:

printf("num1: %d\n", num1);

Perform Arithmetic Operations: Perform some basic arithmetic operations using the integer and floating-point variables. For example:

Add num1 and num2 and print the result.
Multiply float1 and float2 and print the result.
Character Operations: Concatenate char1 and char2 into a single string and print it.

Boolean Output: Display a message based on the value of the isProgrammingFun variable. For example:

if (isProgrammingFun) {
    printf("I find programming fun!\n");
} else {
    printf("Programming is not my thing.\n");
}

User Input: Ask the user to input a new value for one of the variables (e.g., num1) using scanf and then print the updated value.

Challenge: Declare a constant variable PI and initialize it with the value of π (approximately 3.14159). Use this constant to calculate the circumference of a circle with a radius of your choice and print the result.

Remember to include appropriate header files (#include <stdio.h>) and declare your variables with the correct data types before using them. This exercise will help you get hands-on experience with different data types in C and perform basic operations with them.

Here's the solution to the exercise on declaring and initializing variables of different data types in C programming, along with descriptions of each step:

```c
#include <stdio.h>

int main() {
    // Integer Variables
    int num1 = 10; // Declare and initialize num1 with the value 10
    int num2 = 20; // Declare and initialize num2 with the value 20

    // Floating-Point Variables
    float float1 = 3.14;    // Declare and initialize float1 with the value 3.14
    float float2 = 2.718;   // Declare and initialize float2 with the value 2.718

    // Character Variables
    char char1 = 'A';    // Declare and initialize char1 with the character 'A'
    char char2 = 'B';    // Declare and initialize char2 with the character 'B'

    // String Variable
    char name[] = "John Doe";   // Declare and initialize a string variable with your name

    // Boolean Variable
    int isProgrammingFun = 1;   // Declare and initialize a boolean variable (1 for true)

    // Display Values
    printf("num1: %d\n", num1);        // Print the value of num1
    printf("num2: %d\n", num2);        // Print the value of num2
    printf("float1: %f\n", float1);    // Print the value of float1
    printf("float2: %f\n", float2);    // Print the value of float2
    printf("char1: %c\n", char1);      // Print the value of char1
    printf("char2: %c\n", char2);      // Print the value of char2
    printf("name: %s\n", name);        // Print the string stored in the name variable
```

```c
    // Perform Arithmetic Operations
    int sum = num1 + num2;              // Calculate the sum of num1
and num2
    printf("Sum of num1 and num2: %d\n", sum); // Print the result

    float product = float1 * float2;           // Calculate the product of
float1 and float2
    printf("Product of float1 and float2: %f\n", product);  // Print the
result

    // Character Operations
    char combinedChars[3];          // Declare a character array to hold
the combined characters
    combinedChars[0] = char1;       // Assign the value of char1 to the
first element
    combinedChars[1] = char2;       // Assign the value of char2 to the
second element
    combinedChars[2] = '\0';        // Null-terminate the string
    printf("Combined characters: %s\n", combinedChars);  // Print the
combined string

    // Boolean Output
    if (isProgrammingFun) {                    // Check the value of
isProgrammingFun
        printf("I find programming fun!\n");       // If true, print this
message
    } else {
        printf("Programming is not my thing.\n");  // If false, print this
message
    }

    // User Input
    printf("Enter a new value for num1: ");    // Prompt the user for
input
    scanf("%d", &num1);                        // Read and store the new
value in num1
    printf("Updated num1: %d\n", num1);        // Print the updated
value

    // Challenge: Calculate Circumference
    const float PI = 3.14159;                  // Declare and initialize a
constant for PI
    float radius = 5.0;                        // Declare and initialize a radius
value
```

```c
    float circumference = 2 * PI * radius;    // Calculate the
circumference
    printf("Circumference of a circle with radius %.2f: %.2f\n", radius,
circumference); // Print the result
    return 0;
}
```

```
num1: 10
num2: 20
float1: 3.140000
float2: 2.718000
char1: A
char2: B
name: John Doe
Sum of num1 and num2: 30
Product of float1 and float2: 8.534520
Combined characters: AB
I find programming fun!
Enter a new value for num1: 1
Updated num1: 1
Circumference of a circle with radius 5.00: 31.42

Process returned 0 (0x0)    execution time : 21.721 s
Press any key to continue.
```

Figure 1 Example of a console output of the execution of exercise 1

Type the Program shown above into Code::Block, compile and run as done in Day 1.

Day 3: Control Flow

Day 3: Control Flow

Reading Assignment: Flow control in C

Flow control in C refers to the mechanisms and constructs used to manage the order of execution of statements or blocks of code within a C program. It allows you to make decisions, repeat actions, and control the overall flow of your program based on certain conditions. Flow control is essential for creating programs that can perform different tasks under different circumstances. There are primarily three types of flow control in C:

1. Sequential Execution: By default, C programs execute statements in a top-down, sequential order. This means that each statement is executed one after the other in the order they appear in the code.

2. Conditional Execution: Conditional execution allows you to make decisions in your program based on certain conditions. This is typically achieved using `if-else` statements, `switch-case` statements, and the ternary conditional operator (`? :`). Conditional execution allows you to execute different blocks of code depending on whether a specified condition is true or false.

3. Iterative Execution (Loops): Iterative execution, also known as looping, allows you to repeat a block of code multiple times. C provides several loop constructs for this purpose, including `for`, `while`, and `do-while` loops. Loops are used when you want to perform a certain action repeatedly until a specific condition is met or while a condition remains true.

Let's briefly explain each of these flow control constructs in more detail:

1. Sequential Execution:

Sequential execution is the most straightforward type of flow control, where statements are executed one after the other from top to bottom in the order they appear in your code. There is no explicit decision-making or repetition involved in sequential execution.

2. Conditional Execution (if-else and switch-case):

- `if-else` statements: These allow you to execute a block of code if a specified condition is true, and an alternative block if the condition is false.

- `switch-case` statements: These are used for multi-way branching. Based on the value of an expression, the program can jump to different code blocks.

3. Iterative Execution (Loops):

`for` loops: Used when you know the number of iterations in advance. It consists of an initialization step, a condition to check before each iteration, and an update step.

`while` loops: Used when you want to repeat a block of code as long as a certain condition remains true. The condition is checked before entering the loop.

`do-while` loops: Similar to `while` loops, but the condition is checked after the block of code is executed, so the code inside the loop is always executed at least once.

Flow control constructs allow you to create programs that can respond to various input scenarios, handle errors, and perform tasks efficiently by controlling the order in which statements are executed. These constructs are fundamental to programming in C and are essential for writing complex and responsive software.

Reading Assignment: Decision-Making (if-else, switch)

Decision-making is a crucial aspect of programming that allows you to control the flow of your code based on certain conditions. In C programming, you can achieve decision-making using two primary constructs: `if-else` statements and `switch-case` statements. Let's explore both of these constructs in detail:

1. if-else Statements:

The `if-else` statement is used to execute different blocks of code based on whether a specified condition is true or false. It allows you to create branching logic in your program.

Here's the basic syntax of an `if-else` statement:

```
if (condition) {
    // Code to execute if the condition is true
} else {
    // Code to execute if the condition is false
}
```

Example:

```c
#include <stdio.h>

int main() {
    int num;

    printf("Enter a number: ");
    scanf("%d", &num);

    if (num > 0) {
        printf("The number is positive.\n");
    } else if (num < 0) {
        printf("The number is negative.\n");
    } else {
        printf("The number is zero.\n");
    }

    return 0;
}
```

In this example, the program checks whether the entered number is positive, negative, or zero and executes different code blocks accordingly.

2. switch-case Statements:

The `switch-case` statement is used for multi-way branching. It allows you to select one of many code blocks to execute based on the value of an expression.

Here's the basic syntax of a `switch-case` statement:

```c
switch (expression) {
    case constant1:
        // Code to execute when expression equals constant1
        break;
    case constant2:
        // Code to execute when expression equals constant2
        break;
    // More cases...
    default:
```

```
      // Code to execute when none of the cases match
}
```

Example:

```c
#include <stdio.h>

int main() {
   char grade;

   printf("Enter your grade (A, B, C, D, or F): ");
   scanf(" %c", &grade);

   switch (grade) {
      case 'A':
         printf("Excellent!\n");
         break;
      case 'B':
         printf("Good job!\n");
         break;
      case 'C':
         printf("Satisfactory.\n");
         break;
      case 'D':
         printf("Needs improvement.\n");
         break;
      case 'F':
         printf("You failed.\n");
         break;
      default:
         printf("Invalid grade.\n");
   }

   return 0;
}
```

In this example, the program uses `switch-case` to provide feedback based on the entered grade.

Both `if-else` and `switch-case` statements are powerful tools for controlling the flow of your C programs. You can choose the one that best suits your specific needs. `if-else` statements are flexible for complex conditions, while `switch-case` statements are useful for situations where you need to match a value against multiple cases. Proper use of these constructs is essential for creating efficient and responsive programs.

Reading Assignment: Looping Techniques

Looping techniques in programming are essential for repeating a block of code multiple times, often with slight variations or until a specific condition is met. Loops allow you to perform tasks efficiently and can simplify your code significantly. In C programming, there are three primary types of loops: `for`, `while`, and `do-while`. Let's explore these looping techniques in more detail:

1. for Loop:

The `for` loop is used when you know the number of iterations in advance. It consists of three parts: initialization, condition, and update.

```
for (initialization; condition; update) {
    // Code to execute in each iteration
}
```

Here's an example that prints numbers from 1 to 5 using a `for` loop:

```
#include <stdio.h>

int main() {
    for (int i = 1; i <= 5; i++) {
        printf("%d ", i);
    }

    return 0;
}
```

2. while Loop:

The `while` loop is used when you want to repeat a block of code as long as a certain condition remains true. The condition is checked before entering the loop.

```
while (condition) {
    // Code to execute in each iteration
}
```

Example: Printing numbers from 1 to 5 using a `while` loop:

```
#include <stdio.h>

int main() {
    int i = 1;

    while (i <= 5) {
        printf("%d ", i);
        i++;
    }

    return 0;
}
```

3. do-while Loop:

The `do-while` loop is similar to the `while` loop, but the condition is checked after the block of code is executed. This means that the code inside the loop is always executed at least once.

```
do {
    // Code to execute in each iteration
} while (condition);
```

Example: Printing numbers from 1 to 5 using a `do-while` loop:

```c
#include <stdio.h>

int main() {
    int i = 1;

    do {
        printf("%d ", i);
        i++;
    } while (i <= 5);

    return 0;
}
```

Loop Control Statements:

In addition to the basic loop constructs, C provides loop control statements that allow you to modify the behavior of loops:

- `break`: Used to exit a loop prematurely based on a certain condition.
- **`continue`:** Skips the rest of the current iteration and proceeds to the next iteration of the loop.

Example of using `break` to exit a loop:

```c
#include <stdio.h>

int main() {
    for (int i = 1; i <= 10; i++) {
        if (i == 5) {
            break; // Exit the loop when i equals 5
        }
        printf("%d ", i);
    }
```

```
    return 0;
}
```

These looping techniques are fundamental in C programming and are used extensively to implement various algorithms and solve problems. Choosing the right type of loop and using loop control statements wisely can make your code more efficient and readable.

Hand on Exercise 1: Positive or Negative Number

Write a C program that takes an integer as input and determines whether it is a positive or negative number.

Type the Program shown above into Code::Block, compile and run as done in Day 1.

```c
#include <stdio.h>

int main() {
   int num;

   printf("Enter an integer: ");
   scanf("%d", &num);

   if (num > 0) {
      printf("The number is positive.\n");
   } else if (num < 0) {
      printf("The number is negative.\n");
   } else {
      printf("The number is zero.\n");
   }

   return 0;
}
```

```
Enter an integer: -7
The number is negative.

Process returned 0 (0x0)    execution time : 3.926 s
Press any key to continue.
```

Figure 2 Example of a console output of the execution of exercise1

Exercise 3: Calculator

Write a C program for a simple calculator that performs addition, subtraction, multiplication, or division based on user input.

Type the Program shown above into Code::Block, compile and run as done in Day 1.

```c
#include <stdio.h>

int main() {
    char operator;
    double num1, num2, result;
    printf("Enter an operator (+, -, *, /): ");
    scanf(" %c", &operator);
    printf("Enter two numbers: ");
    scanf("%lf %lf", &num1, &num2);
    switch (operator) {
        case '+':
            result = num1 + num2;
            break;
        case '-':
            result = num1 - num2;
            break;
        case '*':
            result = num1 * num2;
            break;
        case '/':
            if (num2 != 0) {
                result = num1 / num2;
            } else {
                printf("Error: Division by zero!\n");
                return 1;  // Exit with an error code
            }
            break;
        default:
            printf("Invalid operator!\n");
            return 1;  // Exit with an error code
    }
    printf("Result: %lf\n", result);

    return 0;
```

}

```
C:\myproject\chero\day3\ex2  ×    +  ∨

Enter an operator (+, -, *, /): +
Enter two numbers: 1
2
Result: 3.000000

Process returned 0 (0x0)   execution time : 14.377 s
Press any key to continue.
```

Figure 3 Example of a console output of the execution of exercise2

Day 4: Functions

Day 4: Function

Reading Assignment: Functions and Modular Programming

C programming is a versatile and powerful language that allows you to write efficient and organized code through the use of functions and modular programming. Functions are blocks of code that perform specific tasks, and modular programming is a technique that involves breaking down a program into smaller, manageable parts. In this guide, we'll explore the fundamentals of functions and modular programming in C.

What is a Function?

A function in C is a self-contained block of code that performs a specific task. Functions are used to divide a program into smaller, more manageable parts, making the code easier to read, maintain, and debug. Functions have a name, a return type, and a set of parameters (also known as arguments).

Here's the basic syntax of a C function:

```
return_type function_name(parameters) {
    // Function body
    // Code to perform a specific task
    // ...
```

return value; // (optional) Return a value of the specified
return_type
}

Let's break down the components of a function:

- `return_type`: This specifies the type of value that the function will return, such as `int`, `float`, `void` (for functions that don't return a value), or a custom data type.

- `function_name`: This is the name of the function, which you can choose. It should be descriptive of the task the function performs.

- `parameters`: These are variables or values that you pass into the function to provide input. Parameters are optional, and a function can have none or multiple parameters.

- `return value`: If the function has a return type other than `void`, it should return a value of that type using the `return` statement.

Defining and Calling Functions

To use a function, you need to define it before calling it. Here's an example of a simple function that adds two numbers:

```
#include <stdio.h>

int add(int a, int b) {
    return a + b;
}

int main() {
    int result = add(5, 3); // Calling the add function
    printf("Sum: %d\n", result);
    return 0;
```

```
}
```

In this example, the `add` function takes two `int` parameters, adds them, and returns the result. In the `main` function, we call `add(5, 3)` and print the result.

Benefits of Modular Programming

Modular programming promotes code reusability and maintainability. By breaking your program into smaller functions, you can:

1. Reusability: Functions can be used multiple times in different parts of your program, reducing code duplication.

2. Readability: Smaller functions are easier to read and understand, making your code more accessible to you and others.

3. Maintenance: When you need to fix a bug or make changes, you can focus on the specific function without affecting the entire program.

4. Testing: Functions are easier to test in isolation, making it simpler to identify and fix issues.

Best Practices

Some best practices for using functions and modular programming in C:

1. Function Names: Choose descriptive names for your functions that indicate their purpose.

2. Parameter Names: Use meaningful parameter names that clarify the function's input.

3. Documentation: Add comments to explain what each function does and how to use it.

4. Separation of Concerns: Each function should have a single, well-defined purpose.

5. Avoid Global Variables: Minimize the use of global variables; instead, pass data through function parameters.

6. Error Handling: Implement error handling within your functions to handle unexpected situations gracefully.

7. Testing: Write test cases for your functions to ensure they work correctly.

In summary, functions and modular programming are essential concepts in C programming. They help you create organized, efficient, and maintainable code. As a beginner, practice using functions to break down your programs into manageable pieces, and you'll become a more proficient C programmer over time.

Hand on Exercise 1: Simple Calculator

Create a C program that defines and calls functions to perform basic arithmetic operations: addition, subtraction, multiplication, and division. Your program should:

Define four functions, one for each arithmetic operation (e.g., add, subtract, multiply, and divide).
Prompt the user to enter two numbers and an operator (+, -, *, or /).
Call the appropriate function based on the operator entered by the user.
Display the result of the operation.

Type the Program shown above into Code::Block, compile and run as done in Day 1.

```
#include <stdio.h>

// Function to check if a number is prime
int isPrime(int n) {
   if (n <= 1) {
      return 0; // 0 and 1 are not prime
   }
   for (int i = 2; i * i <= n; i++) {
      if (n % i == 0) {
         return 0; // Not prime if divisible by any number other than 1
and itself
      }
   }
   return 1; // Prime otherwise
```

```
}

int main() {
    int num;

    printf("Enter a positive integer: ");
    scanf("%d", &num);

    if (num <= 0) {
        printf("Error: Please enter a positive integer.\n");
    } else {
        if (isPrime(num)) {
            printf("%d is a prime number.\n", num);
        } else {
            printf("%d is not a prime number.\n", num);
        }
    }

    return 0;
}
```

C:\myproject\chero\day4\ex1' ✕   + ⌄

```
Enter two numbers: 1 5
Enter an operator (+, -, *, /): +
Result: 6.00

Process returned 0 (0x0)    execution time : 7.729 s
Press any key to continue.
```

Figure 4 Example of a console output of the execution of exercise 1

Exercise 2: Check Prime Numbers

Create a C program that defines a function to check if a given positive integer is prime. Your program should:

Define a function isPrime that takes an integer as a parameter and returns true (1) if it's prime or false (0) otherwise.
Prompt the user to enter a positive integer.
Call the isPrime function to check if the entered number is prime.
Display a message indicating whether the number is prime or not.

Type the Program shown above into Code::Block, compile and run as done in Day 1.

```c
#include <stdio.h>

// Function to calculate factorial
long long calculateFactorial(int n) {
    if (n <= 1) {
        return 1;
    }
    return n * calculateFactorial(n - 1);
}

int main() {
    int num;

    printf("Enter a non-negative integer: ");
    scanf("%d", &num);

    if (num < 0) {
        printf("Error: Please enter a non-negative integer.\n");
    } else {
        long long factorial = calculateFactorial(num);
        printf("Factorial of %d is %lld\n", num, factorial);
    }

    return 0;
}
```

```
C:\myproject\chero\day4\ex2  ×    +  ∨

Enter a positive integer: 11
11 is a prime number.

Process returned 0 (0x0)   execution time : 4.244 s
Press any key to continue.
```

Figure 5 Example of a console output of the execution of exercise2

Exercise 3: Factorial Calculation

Write a C program to calculate the factorial of a non-negative integer using a function. Your program should:

Define a function calculateFactorial that takes an integer as a parameter and returns its factorial.
Prompt the user to enter a non-negative integer.
Call the calculateFactorial function to compute the factorial.
Display the result.

Type the Program shown above into Code::Block, compile and run as done in Day 1.

```
#include <stdio.h>

// Function to generate the first n Fibonacci numbers
void generateFibonacci(int n) {
    int fib1 = 0, fib2 = 1, next;

    printf("Fibonacci Series (first %d numbers):\n", n);

    for (int i = 0; i < n; i++) {
        if (i <= 1) {
            next = i;
        } else {
            next = fib1 + fib2;
            fib1 = fib2;
```

```
        fib2 = next;
    }
    printf("%d ", next);
}
printf("\n");
}

int main() {
    int n;

    printf("Enter the number of Fibonacci numbers to generate: ");
    scanf("%d", &n);

    if (n <= 0) {
        printf("Error: Please enter a positive integer.\n");
    } else {
        generateFibonacci(n);
    }

    return 0;
}
```

Figure 6 Example of a console output of the execution of exercise3

Day 5: Data Types and Operators

Day 5: Data Types and Operators

Reading Assignment: Integers and Floating-Point Numbers

Integers and Floating-Point Numbers in C

In C programming, integers and floating-point numbers are fundamental data types used to represent and manipulate numerical data. Understanding these data types is crucial for beginners as they form the basis for performing mathematical operations and storing numeric values in your programs.

Integers

Integers are whole numbers, and in C, they can be of various sizes depending on the specific data type used. Here are some common integer data types in C:

1. `int`

The `int` data type is the most commonly used integer type in C. It typically represents signed integers, meaning it can hold both positive and negative whole numbers. The size of an `int` can vary depending on the compiler and platform, but it's usually 4 bytes on most systems.

int myInteger = 42;

2. `char`

Although `char` is often used to represent characters, it's essentially a small integer type that can hold integer values ranging from -128 to 127 (or 0 to 255 if unsigned). It occupies 1 byte of memory.

char myChar = 'A';

3. `short` and `long`

`short` and `long` are used to define integers with different storage sizes. `short` typically uses 2 bytes, while `long` usually uses 4 or 8 bytes, depending on the system.

short myShort = 32767;
long myLong = 2147483647;

4. `unsigned` Integers

If you need to represent only non-negative integers, you can use `unsigned` versions of integer types. These types have no sign bit, which means they can represent larger positive values.

unsigned int myUnsignedInt = 12345;

Floating-Point Numbers

Floating-point numbers are used to represent real numbers, including fractional values. In C, there are two primary types for representing floating-point numbers:

1. `float`

The `float` data type is used to represent single-precision floating-point numbers. It typically occupies 4 bytes and can store values with 6-9 significant decimal digits.

float myFloat = 3.14159;

2. `double`

The `double` data type is used to represent double-precision floating-point numbers, providing greater precision compared to `float`. It usually occupies 8 bytes and can store values with 15-18 significant decimal digits.

double myDouble = 3.14159265359;

Example: Using Integers and Floating-Point Numbers

```c
#include <stdio.h>

int main() {
    int myInteger = 42;
    float myFloat = 3.14;

    printf("Integer: %d\n", myInteger);
    printf("Float: %f\n", myFloat);

    return 0;
}
```

In this example, we declare an integer and a floating-point number, and then we use `printf` to display their values.

Remember to choose the appropriate data type based on your program's requirements to avoid unnecessary memory usage or loss of precision. Understanding these fundamental data types is essential for performing mathematical operations and handling numeric data effectively in C programming.

Hand On: Exercise 1 declaration and initialization

Write a C program to declare and initialize variables of different data types (int, float, char, double) and print their values.

Type the Program shown above into Code::Block, compile and run as done in Day 1.

```
#include <stdio.h>

int main() {
    int num1 = 10;
    float num2 = 3.14;
    char letter = 'A';
    double num3 = 5.6789;

    printf("Integer: %d\n", num1);
    printf("Float: %f\n", num2);
    printf("Character: %c\n", letter);
    printf("Double: %lf\n", num3);

    return 0;
}
```

```
Integer: 10
Float: 3.140000
Character: A
Double: 5.678900

Process returned 0 (0x0)   execution time : 1.143 s
Press any key to continue.
```

Figure 7 Example of a console output of the execution of exercise1

Exercise 2 to swap the values of two variables

Write a C program to swap the values of two variables without using a temporary variable.

Type the Program shown above into Code::Block, compile and run as done in Day 1.

```
#include <stdio.h>

int main() {
    int a = 5, b = 10;

    printf("Before swapping: a = %d, b = %d\n", a, b);

    a = a + b;
    b = a - b;
    a = a - b;

    printf("After swapping: a = %d, b = %d\n", a, b);

    return 0;
}
```

```
C:\myproject\chero\day5\ex2   ✕   +  ⌄

Before swapping: a = 5, b = 10
After swapping: a = 10, b = 5

Process returned 0 (0x0)   execution time : 0.868 s
Press any key to continue.
```

Figure 8 Example of a console output of the execution of exercise2

Day 6: Advanced Control Flow

Reading Assignment: Decision-Making (if-else, switch)

Decision-making is a fundamental concept in programming that allows a program to execute different sets of instructions based on certain conditions or criteria. In C, decision-making is typically achieved using `if-else` statements and `switch` statements. This topic explores these constructs in detail and provides examples of how they are used in C programming.

if-else Statements:

The `if-else` statement in C is used to make decisions in your code. It allows you to specify a condition, and based on whether that condition is true or false, different blocks of code will be executed.

```
if (condition) {
  // Code to execute if the condition is true
} else {
  // Code to execute if the condition is false
}
```

Example 1: Checking if a Number is Even or Odd:

```
#include <stdio.h>

int main() {
  int num;
  printf("Enter an integer: ");
  scanf("%d", &num);
```

```c
  if (num % 2 == 0) {
     printf("%d is even.\n", num);
  } else {
     printf("%d is odd.\n", num);
  }

  return 0;
}
```

Example 2: Determining Leap Years:

```c
#include <stdio.h>

int main() {
   int year;
   printf("Enter a year: ");
   scanf("%d", &year);

   if ((year % 4 == 0 && year % 100 != 0) || (year % 400 == 0)) {
      printf("%d is a leap year.\n", year);
   } else {
      printf("%d is not a leap year.\n", year);
   }

   return 0;
}
```

switch Statements:

The `switch` statement in C is another way to make decisions. It allows you to choose between multiple code blocks to execute based on the value of an expression.

```
switch (expression) {
    case constant1:
        // Code to execute if expression equals constant1
        break;
    case constant2:
        // Code to execute if expression equals constant2
        break;
    // ...
    default:
        // Code to execute if expression doesn't match any constant
}
```

Example: Implementing a Calculator with `switch`:

```
#include <stdio.h>

int main() {
    double num1, num2, result;
    char operator;

    printf("Enter two numbers: ");
    scanf("%lf %lf", &num1, &num2);
    printf("Enter an operator (+, -, *, /): ");
    scanf(" %c", &operator);

    switch (operator) {
        case '+':
            result = num1 + num2;
            break;
        case '-':
            result = num1 - num2;
            break;
```

```c
    case '*':
        result = num1 * num2;
        break;
    case '/':
        if (num2 != 0) {
            result = num1 / num2;
        } else {
            printf("Error: Division by zero!\n");
            return 1; // Exit with an error code
        }
        break;
    default:
        printf("Invalid operator\n");
        return 1; // Exit with an error code
    }

    printf("Result: %lf\n", result);

    return 0;
}
```

In summary, decision-making in C programming is crucial for controlling the flow of your program based on specific conditions or input values. `if-else` and `switch` statements provide powerful tools for implementing various decision-making scenarios in your code. Understanding and using these constructs effectively is essential for writing robust and flexible C programs.

Reading Assignment: Looping Techniques

Looping techniques are fundamental in C programming, allowing you to execute a block of code repeatedly until a specified condition is met. There are different types of loops available in C, each with its own use cases and syntax. In this discussion, we'll cover the three primary types of loops in C: `for`, `while`, and `do-while`.

1. `for` Loop:

The `for` loop is used when you know in advance how many times you want to execute a block of code. It consists of three parts: initialization, condition, and increment/decrement.

```
for (initialization; condition; increment/decrement) {
    // Code to execute repeatedly
}
```

Example: Printing Numbers from 1 to 5 using a `for` Loop:

```
#include <stdio.h>

int main() {
    for (int i = 1; i <= 5; i++) {
        printf("%d ", i);
    }
    printf("\n");

    return 0;
```

}

2. `while` Loop:

The `while` loop is used when you want to execute a block of code as long as a certain condition is true. It evaluates the condition before each iteration.

```
while (condition) {
    // Code to execute repeatedly
}
```

Example: Summing Numbers from 1 to 10 using a `while` Loop:

```
#include <stdio.h>

int main() {
    int sum = 0;
    int i = 1;

    while (i <= 10) {
        sum += i;
        i++;
    }

    printf("Sum: %d\n", sum);

    return 0;
}
```

3. `do-while` Loop:

The `do-while` loop is similar to the `while` loop, but it guarantees that the code block is executed at least once because it evaluates the condition after the first iteration.

```
do {
    // Code to execute repeatedly
} while (condition);
```

Example: Reading User Input Until a Valid Number is Entered using a `do-while` Loop:

```
#include <stdio.h>

int main() {
    int num;

    do {
        printf("Enter a positive number: ");
        scanf("%d", &num);
    } while (num <= 0);

    printf("You entered: %d\n", num);

    return 0;
}
```

Loop Control Statements:

In addition to basic looping techniques, C provides loop control statements that allow you to modify the flow of a loop:

- `break`: Terminates the loop prematurely, moving the control outside of the loop.

- `continue`: Skips the current iteration of the loop and continues with the next iteration.

- `goto`: Allows you to jump to a labeled statement within the loop or function. However, the use of `goto` is generally discouraged because it can make code less readable and harder to maintain.

Here's an example using `break` to exit a loop when a condition is met:

```c
#include <stdio.h>

int main() {
    for (int i = 1; i <= 10; i++) {
        if (i == 5) {
            break; // Exit the loop when i is 5
        }
        printf("%d ", i);
    }
    printf("\n");

    return 0;
}
```

In summary, looping techniques are essential for controlling the flow of your C programs when you need to repeat a set of instructions multiple times. Understanding the differences and use cases of `for`, `while`, and `do-while` loops, as well as loop control statements, is crucial for effective C programming.

Hand on Exercise 1: Guess the Number Game

Create a simple "Guess the Number" game in C. The program will generate a random number between 1 and 100, and the user will have to guess the number. The program should provide hints to help the user narrow down their guesses.

Instructions:

Generate a random number between 1 and 100.
Initialize a variable to keep track of the number of guesses.
Implement a loop that allows the user to guess the number until they guess it correctly or reach a maximum number of guesses (e.g., 10).
For each guess, provide feedback to the user:
If the guess is too low, print "Too low. Try again."
If the guess is too high, print "Too high. Try again."
If the guess is correct, print "Congratulations! You guessed the number in X guesses," where X is the number of guesses taken.

If the user exceeds the maximum number of guesses, print "You've run out of guesses. The number was Y," where Y is the correct number.

Type the Program shown above into Code::Block, compile and run as done in Day 1.

```
#include <stdio.h>
#include <stdlib.h>
#include <time.h>

int main() {
    // Seed the random number generator with the current time
    srand(time(NULL));

    // Generate a random number between 1 and 100
    int secretNumber = rand() % 100 + 1;

    int guess;
    int numGuesses = 0;
    int maxGuesses = 10;

    printf("Welcome to the Guess the Number game!\n");
    printf("I have selected a number between 1 and 100.\n");

    while (numGuesses < maxGuesses) {
        printf("Enter your guess: ");
        scanf("%d", &guess);

        numGuesses++;
```

```c
    if (guess < secretNumber) {
        printf("Too low. Try again.\n");
    } else if (guess > secretNumber) {
        printf("Too high. Try again.\n");
    } else {
        printf("Congratulations! You guessed the number in %d guesses.\n",
numGuesses);
        break;
    }
}

if (numGuesses == maxGuesses) {
    printf("You've run out of guesses. The number was %d.\n", secretNumber);
}

return 0;
}
```

C:\myproject\chero\day6\ex1' ✕ + ⌄

```
Welcome to the Guess the Number game!
I have selected a number between 1 and 100.
Enter your guess: 5
Too low. Try again.
Enter your guess: 50
Too low. Try again.
Enter your guess: 75
Too low. Try again.
Enter your guess: 90
Too high. Try again.
Enter your guess: 85
Too low. Try again.
Enter your guess: 90
Too high. Try again.
Enter your guess: 86
Too low. Try again.
Enter your guess: 87
Congratulations! You guessed the number in 8 guesses.

Process returned 0 (0x0)   execution time : 41.740 s
Press any key to continue.
```

Figure 9 Example of a console output of the execution of exercise1

This program uses the rand() function to generate a random number within the specified range. It then uses a while loop to repeatedly ask the user for guesses and provides feedback based on their guesses. If the user guesses the correct number or runs out of guesses, the program displays an appropriate message.

Feel free to modify and expand this program to add more features or challenges to the game.

Hand on exercise 2: Implement complex loop structures.

Write a C program to find the sum of prime numbers within a given range.

Instructions:

Prompt the user to enter a positive integer n as the upper limit of the range.
Implement a loop that iterates from 2 to n. For each number in this range, check if it's prime.
To check if a number is prime, you'll need to use nested loops:
For each number x in the range 2 to the square root of the number you're checking, do the following:
If the number is divisible evenly by x, it's not prime.
If no x in the range divides the number evenly, it's prime.

If a number is prime, add it to a running sum.
After the loop, display the sum of all prime numbers within the range.

Type the Program shown below into Code::Block, compile and run as done in Day 1.

```c
#include <stdio.h>
#include <math.h>

int isPrime(int num) {
    if (num <= 1) {
        return 0; // 0 and 1 are not prime
    }
    if (num <= 3) {
        return 1; // 2 and 3 are prime
    }
    if (num % 2 == 0 || num % 3 == 0) {
        return 0; // Numbers divisible by 2 or 3 are not prime
    }

    // Check for prime using 6k +/- 1 rule
    for (int i = 5; i * i <= num; i += 6) {
        if (num % i == 0 || num % (i + 2) == 0) {
            return 0; // Not prime
        }
    }

    return 1; // Prime
}

int main() {
    int n, sum = 0;

    printf("Enter a positive integer n: ");
    scanf("%d", &n);

    if (n < 2) {
        printf("There are no prime numbers in the specified range.\n");
    } else {
        for (int i = 2; i <= n; i++) {
            if (isPrime(i)) {
```

```
            sum += i;
        }
    }

    printf("The sum of prime numbers from 2 to %d is %d.\n", n, sum);
    }

    return 0;
}
```

```
Enter a positive integer n: 5
The sum of prime numbers from 2 to 5 is 10.

Process returned 0 (0x0)    execution time : 7.180 s
Press any key to continue.
```

Figure 10 Example of a console output of the execution of exercise 2

Day 7: Arrays and Pointers

Day 7: Arrays and Pointers

Reading Assignment: : One-Dimensional Array

One-dimensional arrays are a fundamental concept in the world of C programming. They serve as essential tools for organizing and manipulating data efficiently. An array is a collection of elements of the same data type, stored in contiguous memory locations and identified by a common name. These elements can be accessed individually using an index that represents their position within the array.

One-dimensional arrays are particularly useful when you need to work with a set of related values, such as a list of numbers, characters, or any other data type. They provide a structured way to store and manage multiple pieces of data under a single variable name.

In this introduction to one-dimensional arrays in C, we'll explore how to declare, initialize, access, and manipulate arrays. We'll also delve into common use cases where one-dimensional arrays prove invaluable, from simple tasks like storing a list of exam scores to more complex applications like managing data records.

By understanding the principles of one-dimensional arrays and practicing their usage, you'll gain a solid foundation in C programming that will empower you to solve a wide range of computational problems efficiently and effectively. So, let's begin our journey into the world of one-dimensional arrays in C and unlock their potential for managing and processing data.

Here's a basic example of using a one-dimensional array in C:

```
#include <stdio.h>

int main() {
    // Declare an array of integers with a fixed size of 5
    int numbers[5];

    // Initialize the elements of the array
    numbers[0] = 10;
    numbers[1] = 20;
    numbers[2] = 30;
    numbers[3] = 40;
    numbers[4] = 50;

    // Access and print the elements of the array
    printf("Element at index 0: %d\n", numbers[0]);
    printf("Element at index 1: %d\n", numbers[1]);
    printf("Element at index 2: %d\n", numbers[2]);
    printf("Element at index 3: %d\n", numbers[3]);
    printf("Element at index 4: %d\n", numbers[4]);

    return 0;
}
```

In this example:

1. We include the standard input/output library `stdio.h`.

2. We declare an array called `numbers` capable of holding five integers.

3. We initialize each element of the array with integer values.

4. We access and print each element of the array using their respective indices.

This program declares, initializes, and prints the elements of a one-dimensional integer array. It's a fundamental example to get started with one-dimensional arrays in C. You can modify the size of the array and the values as needed for your specific application.

Reading Assignment: Introduction to Pointers

Pointers are a powerful and fundamental concept in the C programming language, offering a level of control and flexibility that is not easily achievable through other means. Understanding pointers is crucial for every C programmer, as they play a pivotal role in memory management, data manipulation, and interaction with the underlying system.

A pointer is a variable that stores the memory address of another variable. Instead of directly holding data like regular variables (integers, floats, etc.), pointers store the location in memory where data is stored. This ability to reference memory addresses allows C programmers to perform tasks that would otherwise be challenging or impossible.

In this introduction to pointers in C, we'll explore how to declare, initialize, and use pointers effectively. We'll cover various pointer operations, such as dereferencing (accessing the data at a memory address), pointer arithmetic (navigating through memory), and dynamic memory allocation (allocating and freeing memory at runtime).

Pointers are used extensively in C for a wide range of tasks, including:

1. **Dynamic Memory Allocation**: Pointers enable the allocation and deallocation of memory dynamically, allowing programs to adapt to changing data requirements.

2. **Passing Parameters to Functions**: Pointers allow functions to modify variables outside their scope by passing the memory address of those variables.

3. **Arrays and Strings**: Arrays and strings in C are implemented using pointers. Understanding this relationship is essential for efficient manipulation of data.

4. **Data Structures**: Pointers are integral to building complex data structures like linked lists, trees, and graphs.

5. **Efficient I/O Operations**: Pointers are used to optimize file handling and network communication.

6. **Accessing Hardware**: Pointers are used for direct memory access, which is crucial when interacting with hardware devices.

While pointers offer a high degree of control, they also come with challenges, including potential pitfalls like memory leaks and pointer-related errors (e.g., dereferencing a null pointer). Therefore, it's essential to learn pointers gradually, practice diligently, and adopt best practices to write reliable and efficient C programs.

By mastering pointers, you'll unlock the true potential of the C language and gain the ability to write more efficient, flexible, and low-level code, making it a valuable skill for systems programming, embedded systems development, and various other domains. So, let's embark on this journey to understand pointers in C and harness their power in your programming endeavors.

Hand on Exercise 1: array declaration and initialization

Declare an array and print its elements
Write a program that declares an array of integers and initializes it with values. Then, print all the elements of the array.

Type the Program shown below into Code::Block, compile and run as done in Day 1.

```
#include <stdio.h>

int main() {
  // Declare and initialize an array of integers
  int numbers[] = {10, 20, 30, 40, 50};

  // Calculate the size of the array
  int size = sizeof(numbers) / sizeof(numbers[0]);

  // Print the elements of the array
  for (int i = 0; i < size; i++) {
    printf("Element at index %d: %d\n", i, numbers[i]);
  }

  return 0;
}
```

```
Element at index 0: 10
Element at index 1: 20
Element at index 2: 30
Element at index 3: 40
Element at index 4: 50

Process returned 0 (0x0)    execution time : 0.804 s
Press any key to continue.
```

Figure 11 Example of a console output of the execution of exercise 1

Hand on Exercise 2: the sum of array

Write a program that calculates the sum of all elements in an array of integers.

Type the Program shown below into Code::Block, compile and run as done in Day 1.

```
#include <stdio.h>

int main() {
    int numbers[] = {10, 20, 30, 40, 50};
    int size = sizeof(numbers) / sizeof(numbers[0]);
    int sum = 0;

    // Calculate the sum of array elements
    for (int i = 0; i < size; i++) {
        sum += numbers[i];
    }

    printf("Sum of array elements: %d\n", sum);

    return 0;
}
```

```
Sum of array elements: 150

Process returned 0 (0x0)    execution time : 0.741 s
Press any key to continue.
```

Figure 12 Example of a console output of the execution of exercise 2

Exercise 3: Reverse an array

Write a program that reverses the elements of an array of integers in-place.

Type the Program shown below into Code::Block, compile and run as done in Day 1.

#include <stdio.h>

int main() {
*   int numbers[] = {10, 20, 30, 40, 50};*
*   int size = sizeof(numbers) / sizeof(numbers[0]);*

*   // Reverse the array in-place*
*   for (int i = 0; i < size / 2; i++) {*
*   int temp = numbers[i];*
*   numbers[i] = numbers[size - 1 - i];*
*   numbers[size - 1 - i] = temp;*
*   }*

*   // Print the reversed array*
*   for (int i = 0; i < size; i++) {*

```
        printf("Element at index %d: %d\n", i, numbers[i]);
    }

    return 0;
}
```

Figure 13 Example of a console output of the execution of exercise 3

Hand on Exercise 4: Swap Two Integers using Pointers

Write a C program that swaps the values of two integers using pointers.

Type the Program shown below into Code::Block, compile and run as done in Day 1.

```c
#include <stdio.h>

void swap(int *a, int *b) {
    int temp = *a;
    *a = *b;
    *b = temp;
}

int main() {
    int num1 = 5, num2 = 10;

    printf("Before swap: num1 = %d, num2 = %d\n", num1, num2);
    swap(&num1, &num2);
    printf("After swap: num1 = %d, num2 = %d\n", num1, num2);

    return 0;
}
```

```
Before swap: num1 = 5, num2 = 10
After swap: num1 = 10, num2 = 5

Process returned 0 (0x0)   execution time : 0.570 s
Press any key to continue.
```

Figure 14 Example of a console output of the execution of exercise 4

Exercise 5: Find the Length of a String using Pointers

Write a C program that calculates the length of a string using pointers.

Type the Program shown below into Code::Block, compile and run as done in Day 1.

#include <stdio.h>

int stringLength(const char *str) {
    const char *p = str;
    while (*p) {
        p++;
    }
    return p - str;
}

```c
int main() {
    const char *text = "Hello, World!";
    int length = stringLength(text);

    printf("Length of the string: %d\n", length);

    return 0;
}
```

C:\myproject\chero\day7\ex5 ✕ + ⌄

Length of the string: 13

Process returned 0 (0x0)   execution time : 0.725 s
Press any key to continue.

Figure 15 Example of a console output of the execution of exercise 5

Exercise 6: Calculate the Sum of an Array using Pointers

Write a C program that calculates the sum of elements in an array using pointers.

Type the Program shown below into Code::Block, compile and run as done in Day 1.

#include <stdio.h>

int arraySum(int *arr, int size) {
    int sum = 0;
    for (int i = 0; i < size; i++) {
        sum += *(arr + i);

```
    }
    return sum;
}

int main() {
    int numbers[] = {1, 2, 3, 4, 5};
    int size = sizeof(numbers) / sizeof(numbers[0]);
    int sum = arraySum(numbers, size);

    printf("Sum of elements in the array: %d\n", sum);

    return 0;
}
```

C:\myproject\chero\day7\ex6 ✕   + ⌄

```
Sum of elements in the array: 15

Process returned 0 (0x0)    execution time : 0.549 s
Press any key to continue.
```

Figure 16 Example of a console output of the execution of exercise 6

Exercise 7: Pointer Arithmetic with Arrays

Write a C program that demonstrates pointer arithmetic with arrays by printing the elements of an integer array in reverse order using pointers.

Type the Program shown below into Code::Block, compile and run as done in Day 1.

```
#include <stdio.h>

void printReverse(int *arr, int size) {
    int *p = arr + size - 1;
    while (p >= arr) {
```

```
    printf(" % d ", *p);
    p--;
  }
  printf(" \n");
}

int main() {
  int numbers[] = {1, 2, 3, 4, 5};
  int size = sizeof(numbers) / sizeof(numbers[0]);

  printf("Array in reverse order: ");
  printReverse(numbers, size);

  return 0;
}
```

```
C:\myproject\chero\day7\ex7    ×    +   ∨

Array in reverse order: 5 4 3 2 1

Process returned 0 (0x0)    execution time : 0.569 s
Press any key to continue.
```

Figure 17 Example of a console output of the execution of exercise

Day 8: File Handling

Day 8: File Handling

Reading Assignment: File I/O Basics

File I/O (Input/Output) is a fundamental aspect of programming that allows you to read data from and write data to files. In this basic guide, I'll provide examples in C for both reading from and writing to files. You can adapt these concepts to other programming languages as well.

1. Reading from a File

Here's how you can read from a file in C:

```
#include <stdio.h>

int main() {
    // Declare a file pointer
    FILE *file;

    // Open the file for reading
    file = fopen("sample.txt", "r");

    // Check if the file opened successfully
    if (file == NULL) {
        printf("Error opening the file.\n");
        return 1; // Exit with an error code
    }

    // Read and print each line from the file
    char line[100]; // Assuming lines are not longer than 100 characters
    while (fgets(line, sizeof(line), file) != NULL) {
        printf("%s", line);
```

```
    }

    // Close the file
    fclose(file);

    return 0;
}
```

In this example, we:

- Declare a file pointer (`FILE *file`).
- Open the file using `fopen`, specifying the file name ("sample.txt") and the mode ("r" for reading).
- Check if the file opened successfully.
- Use `fgets` to read lines from the file and print them.
- Finally, close the file with `fclose`.

2. Writing to a File

Here's how you can write to a file in C:

```
#include <stdio.h>

int main() {
    // Declare a file pointer
    FILE *file;

    // Open the file for writing
    file = fopen("output.txt", "w");

    // Check if the file opened successfully
    if (file == NULL) {
        printf("Error opening the file.\n");
        return 1; // Exit with an error code
    }

    // Write data to the file
    fprintf(file, "Hello, File I/O!\n");
    fprintf(file, "This is a basic example.\n");

    // Close the file
```

```
    fclose(file);

    return 0;
}
```

In this example, we:

- Declare a file pointer (`FILE *file`).
- Open the file using `fopen`, specifying the file name ("output.txt") and the mode ("w" for writing, which creates a new file or truncates an existing one).
- Check if the file opened successfully.
- Use `fprintf` to write data to the file.
- Finally, close the file with `fclose`.

Remember to handle errors properly, check for file opening success, and close the file when you're done to free up system resources. Additionally, you can explore other modes (e.g., "a" for append) and error handling mechanisms for more robust file I/O operations.

Hand on Exercise 1: Reading Text from a File

Write a C program that reads and prints the contents of a text file named "input.txt" to the console.

Create a text file "input.txt" with "Hello" only. The "input.txt" file need to be in the same directory as the main.c. Type the Program shown below into Code::Block, compile and run as done in Day 1.

```
#include <stdio.h>

int main() {
    FILE *file;
    char ch;

    // Open the file for reading
    file = fopen("input.txt", "r");

    // Check if the file opened successfully
    if (file == NULL) {
        printf("Error opening the file.\n");
        return 1; // Exit with an error code
    }

    // Read and print each character from the file
    while ((ch = fgetc(file)) != EOF) {
        printf("%c", ch);
    }

    // Close the file
    fclose(file);
```

return 0;
}

C:\myproject\chero\day8\ex1' ×   + ∨

```
Hello
Process returned 0 (0x0)    execution time : 0.540 s
Press any key to continue.
```

Figure 18 Example of a console output of the execution of exercise 1

Exercise 2: Writing Text to a File

Write a C program that takes user input and writes it to a text file named "output.txt."

Type the Program shown below into Code::Block, compile and run as done in Day 1.

```
#include <stdio.h>

int main() {
    FILE *file;
    char text[1000];

    // Open the file for writing
    file = fopen("output.txt", "w");

    // Check if the file opened successfully
    if (file == NULL) {
        printf("Error opening the file.\n");
        return 1; // Exit with an error code
    }

    printf("Enter text (Press Enter, and then Ctrl+D or Ctrl+Z to end on most systems):\n");

    // Read user input and write it to the file
    while (fgets(text, sizeof(text), stdin) != NULL) {
        fprintf(file, "%s", text);
    }
```

```
// Close the file
fclose(file);

return 0;
}
```

```
C:\myproject\chero\day8\ex2   ×    +   ∨
Enter text (Press Enter, and then Ctrl+D or Ctrl+Z to end on most systems):
hello
^Z
```

Figure 19 Example of a console output of the execution of exercise 2

Exercise 3: Copying Text from One File to Another

Write a C program that reads the contents of one text file named "source.txt" and writes it to another text file named "destination.txt"

Create a text file "source.txt" with "Hello" only. The "source.txt" file need to be in the same directory as the main.c. Type the Program shown below into Code::Block, compile and run as done in Day 1.

```c
#include <stdio.h>

int main() {
    FILE *sourceFile, *destinationFile;
    char ch;

    // Open the source file for reading
    sourceFile = fopen("source.txt", "r");

    // Check if the source file opened successfully
    if (sourceFile == NULL) {
        printf("Error opening the source file.\n");
        return 1; // Exit with an error code
    }
```

```
// Open the destination file for writing
destinationFile = fopen("destination.txt", "w");

// Check if the destination file opened successfully
if (destinationFile == NULL) {
    printf("Error opening the destination file.\n");
    fclose(sourceFile); // Close the source file before exiting
    return 1; // Exit with an error code
}

// Copy content from the source file to the destination file
while ((ch = fgetc(sourceFile)) != EOF) {
    fputc(ch, destinationFile);
}

// Close both files
fclose(sourceFile);
fclose(destinationFile);

return 0;
}
```

For result, Check that file "source.txt content is the same as "destination.txt".

Day 9: Structures and Unions

Reading Assignment: Defining Structures

In C and C++, a structure is a composite data type that allows you to group together variables of different data types under a single name. Structures are a powerful tool for organizing and managing data. Here's how you define structures:

```
struct structureName {
    dataType member1;
    dataType member2;
    // ...
    dataType memberN;
};
```

- `struct`: The `struct` keyword is used to declare a structure.

- `structureName`: This is the name of the structure type. You can choose any valid identifier as the structure name.

- `dataType`: These are the data types of the structure members. Each member can have a different data type.

- `member1`, `member2`, ..., `memberN`: These are the names of the structure members. You can use any valid identifier as member names.

Example:

Let's define a structure to represent a point in 2D space with `x` and `y` coordinates:

```
struct Point {
    int x;
    int y;
};
```

In this example, we've defined a structure named `Point` with two members: `x` and `y`, both of type `int`. Now you can create variables of this structure type:

```
struct Point p1;
struct Point p2;
```

To access and assign values to the members of a structure, you use the dot (`.`) operator:

```
p1.x = 10;
p1.y = 20;

p2.x = -5;
p2.y = 7;
```

Now `p1` represents the point (10, 20), and `p2` represents the point (-5, 7).

Initializing Structures:

You can also initialize a structure at the time of declaration. Here's how you can do it:

```
struct Point p3 = {30, 40}; // Initializes p3 to (30, 40)
```

You can even use designated initializers to assign values explicitly to specific members:

struct Point p4 = {.x = 50, .y = 60}; // Initializes p4 to (50, 60)

Nested Structures:

Structures can be nested within other structures. This is useful for representing complex data structures. For example:

```
struct Line {
    struct Point start;
    struct Point end;
};
```

In this case, the `Line` structure contains two `Point` structures as members.

Using Typedef:

To simplify the use of structures, you can use `typedef` to create a new type name for a structure. For example:

```
typedef struct {
    int x;
    int y;
} Point;
```

Now you can declare `Point` variables directly without using `struct`:

Point p5;

Defining structures in C and C++ is a fundamental concept, allowing you to create custom data types to represent complex data structures in your programs. They are widely used for organizing and managing data efficiently.

Reading Assignment: Unions

A union in C is a composite data type that allows you to define a structure where multiple variables of different data types share the same memory location. Unlike structures, where all members have their memory allocated separately, in a union, only one member can hold a value at a time. Unions are particularly useful when you need to represent different types of data in the same memory space, saving memory and providing flexibility in your programs. Here's how you define and use unions in C programming:

Defining a Union:

The syntax for defining a union is similar to that of a structure:

```
union unionName {
    dataType member1;
    dataType member2;
    // ...
    dataType memberN;
};
```

- `union`: The `union` keyword is used to declare a union.

- `unionName`: This is the name of the union type.

- `dataType`: These are the data types of the union members. Each member can have a different data type.

- `member1`, `member2`, ..., `memberN`: These are the names of the union members.

Example:

Let's define a union called `Value` that can hold an integer, a float, or a character:

```
union Value {
    int intValue;
    float floatValue;
    char charValue;
};
```

In this example, we've defined a union named `Value` with three members: `intValue`, `floatValue`, and `charValue`.

Accessing Union Members:

To access union members, you use the dot (`.`) operator in the same way you do with structures. However, remember that only one member should be accessed and assigned a value at any given time:

```
union Value data;

data.intValue = 42;      // Assign an integer value
data.floatValue = 3.14;  // Assign a floating-point value

// Accessing a member after another has been assigned is undefined behavior
```

Size of a Union:

The size of a union is determined by the size of its largest member. In the example above, the size of the `Value` union would be the size of an integer because it's the largest member.

Initializing Unions:

You can initialize a union at the time of declaration:

union Value data = {42}; // Initializes the intValue member to 42

Use Cases:

1. Memory-Efficient Storage: Unions are used when you want to store different types of data in the same memory location and only need one of those types at a time, making your program more memory-efficient.

2. Implementing Variant Data: Unions are often used to create variant data types where a single variable can hold values of different data types.

Caution:

When working with unions, it's crucial to keep track of which member is currently valid. Accessing the wrong member can lead to undefined behavior and potential data corruption.

In summary, unions in C provide a way to create flexible data structures that allow multiple data types to share memory. They are especially useful when memory efficiency is essential, and you need to work with variant data types in your programs.

Hand on exercise 1: Define and Initialize a Structure

n this exercise, you will define a structure to represent a point in 2D space with x and y coordinates. Then, you will initialize a few point structures and print their values.

Type the Program shown below into Code::Block, compile and run as done in Day 1.

```c
#include <stdio.h>

// Define a structure for a 2D point
struct Point {
    int x;
    int y;
};

int main() {
    // Initialize two Point structures
    struct Point p1 = { 3, 4 };
    struct Point p2 = { -1, 2 };

    // Print the values of the points
    printf("Point 1: (%d, %d)\n", p1.x, p1.y);
    printf("Point 2: (%d, %d)\n", p2.x, p2.y);

    return 0;
}
```

```
Point 1: (3, 4)
Point 2: (-1, 2)

Process returned 0 (0x0)   execution time : 0.769 s
Press any key to continue.
```

Figure 20 Example of a console output of the execution of exercise 1

Exercise 2: Create an Array of Structures

In this exercise, you will create an array of structures to represent a list of students, each with a name and an age. Initialize the array and print the details of each student.

Type the Program shown below into Code::Block, compile and run as done in Day 1.

```
#include <stdio.h>

// Define a structure for a student
struct Student {
    char name[50];
    int age;
};

int main() {
    // Initialize an array of students
    struct Student students[3] = {
        { "Alice", 20 },
        { "Bob", 22 },
        { "Charlie", 19 }
    };

    // Print the details of each student
    for (int i = 0; i < 3; i++) {
```

```
        printf("Student %d:\n", i + 1);
        printf("Name: %s\n", students[i].name);
        printf("Age: %d\n", students[i].age);
        printf("\n");
    }

    return 0;
}
```

```
C:\myproject\chero\day9\ex2   ×   +   ∨
Student 1:
Name: Alice
Age: 20

Student 2:
Name: Bob
Age: 22

Student 3:
Name: Charlie
Age: 19


Process returned 0 (0x0)    execution time : 0.597 s
Press any key to continue.
```

Figure 21 Example of a console output of the execution of exercise 2

Exercise 3: Pass a Structure to a Function

In this exercise, you will define a function that takes a structure as an argument and prints its values. You will then call this function to display the details of a point.

```c
#include <stdio.h>

// Define a structure for a 2D point
struct Point {
    int x;
    int y;
};

// Function to print the details of a Point structure
void printPoint(struct Point p) {
    printf("Point: (%d, %d)\n", p.x, p.y);
}

int main() {
    // Initialize a Point structure
    struct Point p = { 5, 7 };

    // Call the function to print the point
    printPoint(p);

    return 0;
```

}

```
Point: (5, 7)

Process returned 0 (0x0)    execution time : 0.409 s
Press any key to continue.
```

exercise 3Figure 22 Example of a console output of the execution of

These exercises should give you a good starting point for understanding and using structures in your programming language of choice. Structures are essential for organizing and working with complex data in many programming tasks.

Day 10: Advance Topics

Day 10: Advance Topics

Reading Assignment: Preprocessor Directives

Preprocessor directives are an essential component of many programming languages, including C, C++, and assembly language. They are special instructions that are processed by the preprocessor before the actual compilation of code begins. Preprocessor directives are used to provide instructions to the compiler regarding how to preprocess the source code. They don't belong to the core programming language but serve to enhance code readability, maintainability, and portability. Here, we'll focus on the C and C++ programming languages, where preprocessor directives are commonly used.

Here are some commonly used preprocessor directives and their purposes:

1. **#include**: The `#include` directive is used to include header files or other source code files into your program. This is essential for code modularization and reusability. For example:

#include <stdio.h>

2. #define: The `#define` directive is used to define macros, which are like small code snippets that are replaced with their defined values during preprocessing. This can be used for constants or simple functions. For example:

#define PI 3.14159265359

3. #ifdef / #ifndef / #endif: These directives are used for conditional compilation. They allow you to include or exclude certain sections of code based on conditions. For example:

```c
#ifdef DEBUG
// Debugging code here
#endif
```

4. #ifdef / #ifndef / #else / #endif: These directives work together to provide conditional compilation with an alternative branch. If a condition is met, the code between `#ifdef` and `#else` is included; otherwise, the code between `#else` and `#endif` is included. For example:

```c
#ifdef DEBUG
// Debugging code here
#else
// Production code here
#endif
```

5. #pragma: The `#pragma` directive is used to provide compiler-specific instructions or hints. These instructions can vary between different compilers and are typically used for fine-tuning compiler behavior. For example:

#pragma warning(disable: 4996) // Disable a specific compiler warning

6. #error: The `#error` directive is used to generate an error message during preprocessing. This can be helpful for enforcing coding standards or ensuring that certain conditions are met before compilation. For example:

```
#ifdef LINUX
// Linux-specific code
#else
#error This code requires a Linux environment
#endif
```

7. #undef: The `#undef` directive is used to undefine a previously defined macro. This can be useful for selectively disabling macros. For example:

```
#define DEBUG // Enable debugging
// ...
#undef DEBUG // Disable debugging
```

Preprocessor directives play a crucial role in C and C++ programming by allowing developers to write more flexible and portable code. However, they should be used judiciously to avoid code that is difficult to understand and maintain.

Reading Assignment: Bit Manipulation

Bit manipulation in C involves performing various operations on individual bits within data using bitwise operators. Here are some common bit manipulation operations in C:

1. Bitwise AND (`&`)

This operation sets a bit to 1 if it's 1 in both operands.

unsigned int a = 5;   // Binary: 0101
unsigned int b = 3;   // Binary: 0011
unsigned int result = a & b;   // Binary: 0001 (1 in decimal)

2. Bitwise OR (`|`):

This operation sets a bit to 1 if it's 1 in either operand.

unsigned int a = 5;   // Binary: 0101
unsigned int b = 3;   // Binary: 0011
unsigned int result = a | b;   // Binary: 0111 (7 in decimal)

3. Bitwise XOR (`^`):

This operation sets a bit to 1 if it's 1 in one operand but not both.

unsigned int a = 5;   // Binary: 0101
unsigned int b = 3;   // Binary: 0011
unsigned int result = a ^ b;   // Binary: 0110 (6 in decimal)

4. Bitwise NOT (`~`):

This operation flips the bits of a number (1s become 0s, and vice versa).

unsigned int a = 5; // Binary: 0101
unsigned int result = ~a; // Binary: 1010 (4294967290 in decimal)

5. Left Shift (`<<`):

This operation shifts the bits of a number to the left by a specified number of positions.

unsigned int a = 5; // Binary: 0000 0101
unsigned int result = a << 2; // Binary: 0001 0100 (20 in decimal)

6. Right Shift (`>>`):

This operation shifts the bits of a number to the right by a specified number of positions.

unsigned int a = 16; // Binary: 0001 0000
unsigned int result = a >> 2; // Binary: 0000 0100 (4 in decimal)

These bitwise operators can be used for various purposes, such as setting and clearing individual bits, working with hardware registers, and optimizing code for memory usage. Additionally, bit manipulation is often used for tasks like encoding and decoding data structures and implementing efficient algorithms. When working with bit manipulation in C, it's essential to consider data types, signed vs. unsigned values, and potential overflow or unintended side effects.

Exercise 1: Bit Manipulation in C

In this hands-on exercise, you will work with bit manipulation operations in the C programming language. The exercise covers the following key operations:

1. **Bitwise AND:** Perform a bitwise AND operation between two unsigned integers.
2. **Bitwise OR:** Perform a bitwise OR operation between two unsigned integers.
3. **Bitwise XOR:** Perform a bitwise XOR operation between two unsigned integers.
4. **Bitwise NOT:** Perform a bitwise NOT operation on an unsigned integer.
5. **Left Shift:** Left shift the bits of an unsigned integer by a specified number of positions.
6. **Right Shift:** Right shift the bits of an unsigned integer by a specified number of positions.

The exercise provides a C program that demonstrates these operations and prints both the binary and decimal representations of the results. By completing this exercise, you will gain practical experience with fundamental bit manipulation techniques commonly used in low-level programming and embedded systems development.

Type the Program shown below into Code::Block, compile and run as done in Day 1.

```c
#include <stdio.h>

// Function to print the binary representation of an unsigned integer
void printBinary(unsigned int num) {
    if (num > 1)
        printBinary(num >> 1); // Recursive call, shift right
    printf("%d", num & 1); // Print the least significant bit
}

int main() {
    unsigned int num1 = 18; // Binary: 010010
    unsigned int num2 = 9;  // Binary: 001001

    // 1. Perform a bitwise AND operation between num1 and num2.
    unsigned int resultAnd = num1 & num2;
    printf("Bitwise AND: ");
    printBinary(resultAnd);
    printf(" (Decimal: %u)\n", resultAnd);

    // 2. Perform a bitwise OR operation between num1 and num2.
    unsigned int resultOr = num1 | num2;
    printf("Bitwise OR: ");
    printBinary(resultOr);
    printf(" (Decimal: %u)\n", resultOr);

    // 3. Perform a bitwise XOR operation between num1 and num2.
    unsigned int resultXor = num1 ^ num2;
    printf("Bitwise XOR: ");
    printBinary(resultXor);
    printf(" (Decimal: %u)\n", resultXor);

    // 4. Perform a bitwise NOT operation on num1.
    unsigned int resultNot = ~num1;
    printf("Bitwise NOT on num1: ");
    printBinary(resultNot);
    printf(" (Decimal: %u)\n", resultNot);
```

```
// 5. Left shift num1 by 2 positions.
unsigned int resultLeftShift = num1 << 2;
printf("Left Shift by 2: ");
printBinary(resultLeftShift);
printf(" (Decimal: %u)\n", resultLeftShift);

// 6. Right shift num2 by 1 position.
unsigned int resultRightShift = num2 >> 1;
printf("Right Shift by 1: ");
printBinary(resultRightShift);
printf(" (Decimal: %u)\n", resultRightShift);

    return 0;
}
```

```
📝 C:\myproject\chero\day10\ex   ×   +   ∨
Bitwise AND: 0 (Decimal: 0)
Bitwise OR: 11011 (Decimal: 27)
Bitwise XOR: 11011 (Decimal: 27)
Bitwise NOT on num1: 11111111111111111111111111101101 (Decimal: 4294967277)
Left Shift by 2: 1001000 (Decimal: 72)
Right Shift by 1: 100 (Decimal: 4)

Process returned 0 (0x0)   execution time : 0.576 s
Press any key to continue.
```

Figure 23 Example of a console output of the execution of exercise 3

This program performs various bit manipulation operations on `num1` and `num2`, including bitwise AND, OR, XOR, NOT, left shift, and right shift. It also prints both the binary and decimal representations of the results.

Compile and run the program to observe the effects of these bit manipulation operations. This exercise will help you become more comfortable with working on bit-level operations in C.

www.ingramcontent.com/pod-product-compliance
Lightning Source LLC
LaVergne TN
LVHW051654050326
832903LV00032B/3809